skateboarding

ben powell

A CONNECTIONS · AXIS EDITION

A Connections • Axis Edition

This edition first published in Great Britain by
Connections Book Publishing Limited
St Chad's House
148 King's Cross Road
London WC1X 9DH
and Axis Publishing Limited
8c Accommodation Road
London NW11 8ED
www.axispublishing.co.uk

Conceived and created by
Axis Publishing Limited

Creative Director: Siân Keogh
Managing Editor: Brian Burns
Design: Axis Design Editions
Editors: Charlotte Stock and Conor Kilgallon
Production Manager: Sue Bayliss
Production Controller: Juliet Brown
Photographer: Mike Good

Text and images copyright
© Axis Publishing Limited 2003

Note
The opinions and advice expressed in this book are
intended as a guide only. The publisher and author accept
no responsibility for any injury or loss sustained as a
result of using this book.

British Library Cataloguing-in-Publication data available on
request.

ISBN 1–85906–119–2

9 8 7 6 5 4 3 2 1

Printed by Star Standard (Pte) Limited

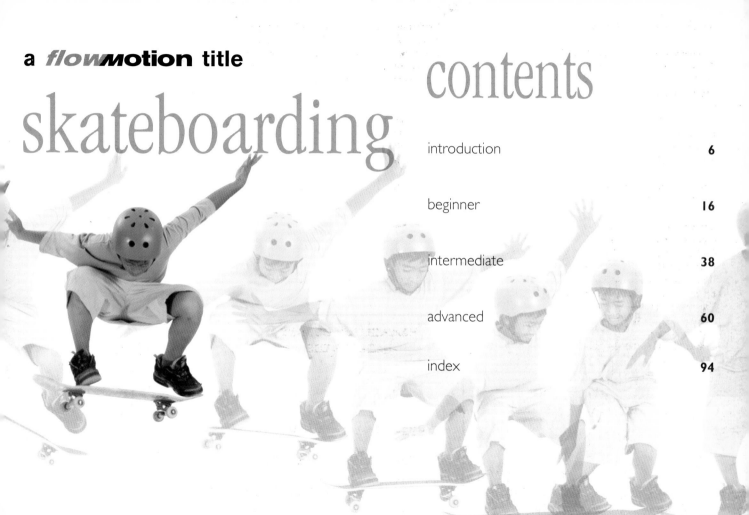

a _flowmotion_ title

skateboarding

contents

introduction

Just when you get to thinking that you've finally found the limits of what can be done on a skateboard, or of what places are left to be found, something new inevitably turns up again to broaden the imagination and boggle the mind.

WARREN BOLSTER, "DESERT DISCOVERY", SKATEBOARDER, VOL. 3, NO. 6 (JULY 1977)

You might imagine that you already know what skateboarding is when you pick up this book. You have seen professional skateboarding on mainstream television and have witnessed the tricks that can be performed on a skateboard; you may even have played a computer game that promises to reveal the secrets of skateboarding to the uninitiated. No matter where you first encountered the ubiquitous wooden plank on wheels, only one thing is certain: without the experience of actually riding a skateboard down a busy street, threading your path through the crowds and traffic while surrounded by the noises of the city, you have absolutely no idea what it means to be a skateboarder.

Skateboarding is everything and nothing. It can become your whole life or it can be nothing more significant than a cheap and enjoyable form of transport. It all depends on the limits of your imagination.

history

Skateboards were first recorded in the mid-1950s and originated from the warm Californian beach towns of the United States. The earliest skateboards would seem extremely primitive to today's skaters. These rudimentary boards were really the ramshackle offspring of a marriage between box-car racers and crude dry-land surfboards. The boards were much smaller than their modern counterparts: the trucks did not have the capacity to turn and the wheels were one-piece affairs made from either clay or metal. Although the basic principle of "travelling without moving", which underlies skateboarding to this day, was evident in these early boards, the ride was much more limited and basic than that enjoyed by modern skaters.

Early bands of skateboarders were only found in a handful of surf communities in the United States until the 1970s when several toy manufacturers discovered the emerging "skateboard craze" and started to mass-manufacture skateboards for the first time. Interest in skateboarding boomed in the mid-1970s as the media began to report on this new sport and photographs of skateboarders started to appear in advertisements and newspapers across the world. As the boom set in, custom-built skateparks began to spring up to accommodate the needs of the skateboarders by providing monitored replicas of the banks and slopes of the streets.

Skateboarding quickly became a massively profitable business and with that came all the trappings of popularity – competitions, champions, professionals and various endorsed products. In just two decades, skateboarding had leapt in status from a home-made hobby to a semi-legitimate sport; it looked set to take the entire world by storm. Unfortunately, the profit-driven direction of the early boom also served to provide the stage for the great crash that befell skateboarding at the end of the 1970s. Badly designed skateparks and inadequate safety equipment led to a wave of lawsuits and park closures. By 1980 (only five years after the great boom), skateboarding was officially declared dead.

back to its roots

In truth, skateboarding did not die. The remaining groups of committed skaters moved out of the spotlight and back to the streets and backyard pools from which they had originally emerged. As most major sports manufacturers ceased making skateboards after the boom ended, skaters were forced to start small companies and set about making their own equipment. Innovations in the design of basic skateboard components came to light during this period as skateboarders themselves began improving performance to enhance their own participation in the sport. Along with this phase of technical innovation came a decade of exploration and invention in terms of the ways that the skateboard could be manipulated by the skater. Most of the tricks featured in this book were invented during this underground period of skateboarding's history, from the mid-1980s to the latter part of the 1990s.

Ironically, the great crash served to concentrate small pockets of hardcore skaters and gave them the freedom to discover the potential of skateboarding, rather than killing it. Freed from the conventions of custom-built environments and competition, skateboarding became the amorphous, shifting sub-culture that it is today and not the clean cut "sport" envisaged by the entrepreneurs of the first boom.

And so we arrive at the present day. Skateboarding is everywhere and has finally regained the levels of exposure and popularity that it last enjoyed for a brief moment in the mid-1970s. Skateboarding may be new to you but behind it lies a long and complex history, albeit one that is largely undocumented outside of specialist magazines. The experiences of this history have created skateboarding as it stands today: neither a sport nor a pastime, neither an art form nor a child's game, but an activity with millions of participants and liberated from any rules whatsoever. Skateboarding just is: all you have to do is get on one and roll. It makes much more sense then. Just enjoy it.

important terms

stances

There are two types of stance in skateboarding: regular-footed and goofy-footed. These are terms that originate from surfing and relate to the foot that you lead with while skating. Regular-footers ride with their left foot at the front of their boards; goofy-footers stand with their right foot forwards. One stance will feel more natural than the other as nature seems to attribute a stance in the same way that some people are left-handed and others are right-handed.

frontside and backside

As with the names of the stances, frontside and backside are surf-derived terms to describe the direction of movement of skaters. Frontside means any trick or movement where

REGULAR   **GOOFY**

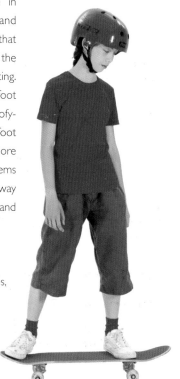

skaters face towards their direction of travel. Backside refers to any trick or movement where skaters face away from their direction of travel.

To comprehend these two terms, it helps to imagine that you are a surfer on a wave. If you turn at the crest facing into the wave, then you are turning in a frontside direction. If you turn with your back facing the crest of the wave, then the direction is described as backside.

switchstance

One of the most unique innovations within skateboarding was the introduction of the idea that skaters could fully master their "unnatural" stance so as to be able to skate equally well with either foot leading. The concept of switch-skating did not exist until the early 1990s. Various professional street skaters of the day (Mark Gonzales, Natas

Kaupas, Mike Carrol and Henry Sanchez among many others) decided to re-invent skateboarding by announcing on skate videos that it was good to learn to skate both ways. Switchstance is one example of the fundamental flexibility inherent in skateboarding and serves to remind all skaters, whether beginner or expert, that the possibilities within this great pastime are almost limitless.

SOME SKATEBOARDING TERMS

A
ACID DROP: Skating off the end of an object with ollieing or touching the board with your hands.

B
BONED: Pushing the board out in front and pointing downwards. Performed in mid-air.

C
CASPER: With the board upside down, place the front foot underneath the board and backfoot on the tail, pointing the board into the sky.

D
DELAM: Damaging a deck by chipping off a layer of plywood. The thin layer removed is called a "delam" and the name is also given to the mark left where the layer once was.

F
FAKIE: The name given to travelling backwards on your skateboard.

FAT: Meaning high or far. Used to express a skateboarding trick that is performed over a long distance or to a great height. Also spelt "Phat".

H
HANDPLANT: A form of handstand where the board is held in the air either by a hand or by feet.

I
IMPOSSIBLE: A freestyle trick invented by Rodney Mullen. Consists of spinning the board around either foot.

J
JAM: Getting lots of skaters together for a skateboarding session.

K
KINK: A term used to describe handrails. The kink is a change in the angle of a handrail. A handrail that runs down a set of steps then becomes horizontal is a two kink rail.

M
McTWIST: A 540-degree backside air with a mute grab. Invented by Mike McGill.

Q
QUARTERPIPE: One side of a mini-ramp or vert ramp, usually with less width and found at skateparks. Often used for gaining speed on a street course or practising ramp tricks.

R
ROCKANDROLL: A ramp trick. Go up to the lip and push the front truck over it. Stall, then turn 180 back down the ramp.

skateboard components

The basic make-up of the skateboard has hardly changed in the last 30 years. Individual components have been refined and updated but the four fundamentals of board, trucks, wheels and bearings have remained constant throughout.

skateboard or "deck"

Most skateboards are made from laminated sheets of plywood using epoxy resins to cement the layers together. The kicktails and concave of the board are produced using moulds at skateboard factories. Most modern skateboards are about 78cm (31in) long and between 18cm and 20cm (7in and 8in) wide. Most of them will be fairly symmetrical in shape, with nose and kicktails to facilitate regular and switch-skating.

wheels

Skateboard wheels are made from polyurethane and come in various diameters and hardness readings. Soft wheels give more grip whereas hard wheels slide more easily on the ground and allow skaters to slide from one direction to other at will. The hardness is determined by a durometer reading. Most street wheels will be somewhere between 90a and 110a on the durometer with slalom or downhill wheels coming in at a softer 65a to 85a.

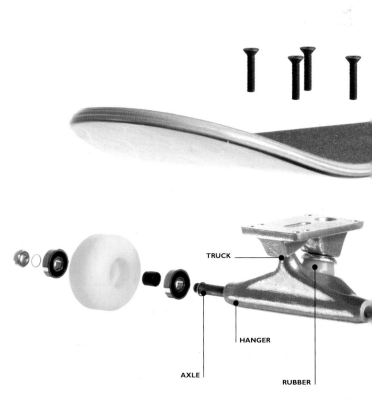

TRUCK

HANGER

AXLE

RUBBER

trucks

These are the metal axles to which the wheels are attached and that allow the skateboard to be turned while moving. Trucks are comprised of:

- **HANGERS:** Metal grinding edge that houses the axle to which the wheels are attached.
- **BASEPLATE:** Metal seat that houses the hanger.
- **KINGPIN:** Threaded bar that holds the hanger in the baseplate.
- **RUBBERS:** Urethane grommets that surround the kingpin and allow the board to turn from side to side.

bearings

These are metal rings filled with tiny ball bearings that fit inside your wheels and allow them to turn. Skate bearings share an identical diameter but various grades and qualities exist.

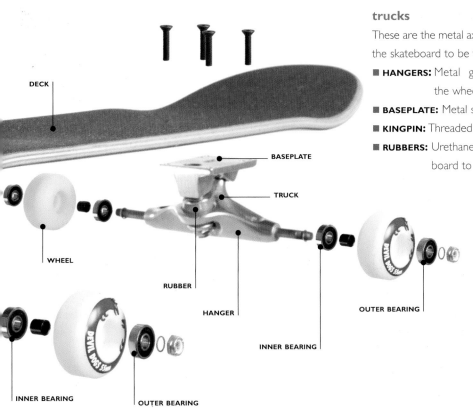

DECK

BASEPLATE

TRUCK

WHEEL

RUBBER

HANGER

OUTER BEARING

INNER BEARING

INNER BEARING

OUTER BEARING

skateboarding and safety

Skateboarding can be very dangerous for both beginners and experienced skaters alike because of its very nature. Although precautions can be taken, such as wearing safety equipment, certain common injuries are an unavoidable part of the learning process. All you can do is minimise their severity by observing a few simple rules.

First, all beginners should choose somewhere suitable to learn the basics. Find somewhere quiet and flat to begin with and concentrate on mastering basic board control before attempting any of the tricks described in this book. Do not go to skateparks until you have a degree of board control as a busy park is not the place to learn how to push and turn. If you follow this simple advice you will avoid one of the major causes of injury among inexperienced skaters.

Second, you need to be aware of the most common injuries and of ways to deal with them. Aside from the obvious cuts and bruises, three main areas of the body are susceptible to injury:

ANKLES: The most common of all skater injuries is the "tweaked ankle". This occurs when skaters fall with the majority of their body weight on the side of their foot and the ankle is hyper-extended. Elevate and ice a tweaked ankle to bring out the bruising and swelling and stay off the injured foot until the bruising and stiffness has gone. This process can take time but you must give your muscles adequate time to heal.

KNEES: This is another problem area and the knees should be protected with knee pads and/or knee gaskets.

WRISTS: Your wrists will take some punishment, especially during your initial learning period. Wrist guards will protect you from twists and breaks.

safety gear

There are four main pieces of safety equipment that are designed to protect those parts of your body most likely to get injured while skateboarding. Although most professionals choose not to use safety equipment, it is probably a good idea for beginners to use at least one of the four main pieces of gear. It will be up to you to

The most important piece of equipment after the skateboard, good skate shoes should provide gripping heels and cushioning for your heels.

decide which is most suitable. However, avoid full padding if you can as it will impede your movement and make it difficult to learn at an early stage. Wrist guards and knee pads are probably the only pieces of safety equipment that you will need while mastering the basics but that is only a suggestion, not a rule.

helmets: Probably the most important piece of equipment as it protects your brains. Choose a helmet that fits correctly, has a solid foam lining and a chin strap that holds it on securely. Most authentic skateboard shops will offer a selection of good quality helmets.

knee pads: Along with wrist guards, knee pads are the most often used pieces of safety gear. They are neoprene-backed and slip over your feet and fasten with velcro straps around the backs of your knees. There should be a plastic cup over your kneecap which allows you to slide out of falls rather than taking all the impact on your knees.

elbow pads: Smaller versions of knee pads that protect your elbows in the same way. These are only really necessary if you are skating big ramps or concrete transitions. Make sure they fit correctly.

wrist guards: These are braces that fit over your wrists and are worn by many skaters, including professionals. Wrist guards stop you from twisting your wrists if you slam and can help protect weak wrists from further injury.

When buying safety equipment, select reliable brands. Make sure that all padding fits securely and is held in place with adjustable straps.

common sense

- Choose your skate spots carefully
- Never skate near roads or traffic
- Never skate in street spots during the day or when there are members of the public around
- Find somewhere quiet and smooth to learn
- Find your local skatepark and use the beginner area before moving out onto bigger obstacles

- If skateboarding is prohibited outside certain buildings or you are asked to move on by security guards, then do so politely
- Use safety equipment where necessary and be aware of your limits
- Skateboard safely
- Some states and many localities have laws regulating skateboarding and the use of safety equipment in skate parks, especially publicly owned ones. Before skating, check the regulations in your state or locality.

go with the flow

The special Flowmotion images used in this book have been created to ensure that you see the whole movement – not just isolated highlights. Each of the image sequences flows across the page in both directions, demonstrating how the technique progresses and how to get into and make the most of each trick safely and effectively. Each technique is also fully explained with step-by-step captions. Below this, another layer of information in the timeline breaks the move into its various key stages, with instructions for the different movements you should make. The symbols in the timeline also include instructions for when to pause for a moment and when to move seamlessly from one stage to the next.

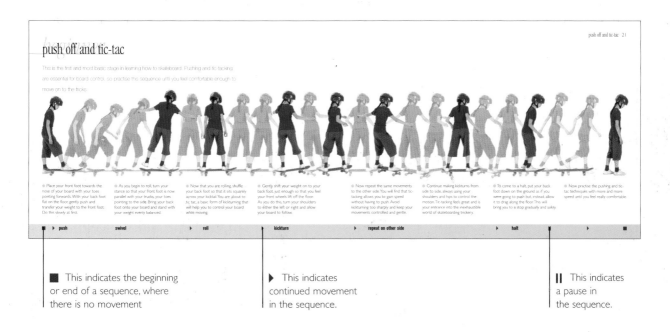

push off and tic-tac 21

push off and tic-tac

This is the first and most basic stage in learning how to skateboard. Pushing and tic-tacking are essential for board control, so practise this sequence until you feel comfortable enough to move on to the tricks.

■ Place your front foot towards the nose of your board with your toes pointing forwards. With your back foot flat on the floor gently push and transfer your weight to the front foot. Do this slowly at first.

● As you begin to roll, turn your stance so that your front foot is now parallel with your trucks, your toes pointing to the side. Bring your back foot onto your board and stand with your weight evenly balanced.

● Now that you are rolling, shuffle your back foot so that it sits squarely across your kicktail. You are about to tic tac, a basic form of kickturning that will help you to control your board while moving.

● Gently shift your weight on to your back foot, just enough so that you feel your front wheels lift off the floor. As you do this, turn your shoulders to either the left or right and allow your board to follow.

● Now repeat the same movements to the other side. You will find that tic-tacking allows you to gain speed without having to push. Avoid kickturning too sharply and keep your movements controlled and gentle.

● Continue making kickturns from side to side, always using your shoulders and hips to control the motion. Tic-tacking feels great and is your entrance into the inexhaustible world of skateboarding trickery.

● To come to a halt, put your back foot down on the ground as if you were going to push but, instead, allow it to drag along the floor. This will bring you to a stop gradually and safely.

● Now practise the pushing and tic-tac techniques with more and more speed until you feel really comfortable.

■ ▶ push   swivel   ▶ roll   kickturn   ▶ repeat on other side   ▶ halt   ▶ ■

■ This indicates the beginning or end of a sequence, where there is no movement

▶ This indicates continued movement in the sequence.

❙❙ This indicates a pause in the sequence.

beginner

powerslide

The powerslide can be used to check your speed and to stop your skateboard. It is the best way of slowing down, since scraping your back foot along the ground when rolling at high speed ruins your skate shoes.

● Roll along at a moderate speed. Take the weight off your front wheels slightly and make the motion of a kickturn but without lifting your wheels off the floor. You have to force your wheels to slide here, so be firm.

● As you start to turn, bend your knees slightly and lean backwards. The aim is to slide your wheels through 90 degrees and then allow your momentum to force you to skid sideways on.

● Lean back slightly, but not too much or you will fall. Using your outstretched arms for balance, slide forwards as your wheels skid along the ground.

● As you feel your slide slowing down, begin to turn your shoulders to prepare to return to a normal rolling position. You will need to transfer your weight from the sliding position so that your body weight is centred again.

● Slide your front wheels back to their original position and continue rolling at a slower speed. You will find that powerslides are much easier to do when you are travelling fast.

● Roll along and prepare yourself to repeat the move with more speed. Powerslides feel incredible and, once mastered, will make you a much more competent skater.

● Congratulate yourself on what you have just accomplished. You now have the know-how to break your speed without ruining your shoes.

▶ **slide**   ▶ **slow**   ▶ **roll**   ▶

push off and tic-tac

This is the first and most basic stage in learning how to skateboard. Pushing and tic-tacking are essential for board control, so practise this sequence until you feel comfortable enough to move on to the tricks.

● Place your front foot towards the nose of your board with your toes pointing forwards. With your back foot flat on the floor, gently push and transfer your weight to the front foot. Do this slowly at first.

● As you begin to roll, turn your stance so that your front foot is now parallel with your trucks, your toes pointing to the side. Bring your back foot onto your board and stand with your weight evenly balanced.

● Now that you are rolling, shuffle your back foot so that it sits squarely across your kicktail. You are about to tic tac, a basic form of kickturning that will help you to control your board while moving.

● Gently shift your weight on to your back foot, just enough so that you feel your front wheels lift off the floor. As you do this, turn your shoulders to either the left or right and allow your board to follow.

 ▶ **push**   **swivel**   ▶ **roll**   ▶ **kickturn**

● Now repeat the same movements to the other side. You will find that tic-tacking allows you to gain speed without having to push. Avoid kickturning too sharply and keep your movements controlled and gentle.

● Continue making kickturns from side to side, always using your shoulders and hips to control the motion. Tic-tacking feels great and is your entrance into the inexhaustible world of skateboarding trickery.

● To come to a halt, put your back foot down on the ground as if you were going to push but, instead, allow it to drag along the floor. This will bring you to a stop gradually and safely.

● Now practise the pushing and tic-tac techniques with more and more speed until you feel really comfortable.

▶ **repeat on other side**　　　　　　▶　**halt**　　**❚❚**　　▶　　■

manual

The manual roll, or "wheelie", is a key building block for more advanced skateboard tricks. Start with manual rolls (on the back wheels) as nose manuals require more balance and board control.

● As you begin to slow down, transfer your weight back towards your rear foot and gently lower your back wheels onto the ground again. Stay balanced on your board.

● Lock yourself into the nose-manual stance with your arms and hips. Look at the ground in front of you and concentrate on keeping your balance centred. Enjoy the feeling for as long as you have speed.

● Place your front foot in the centre of your nose and your back foot on the tail. Shift your weight to your front foot without pressing the nose too heavily. As your back wheels lift off the floor, extend your arms and balance.

● Approach the nose-manual with a little less speed than with the basic manual roll at first. Remember that if you scrape the nose while trying to wheelie along, you will be thrown forwards off your deck onto the floor.

● As you begin to slow down, transfer your weight back towards your front foot and allow your front wheels to descend slowly. Land with all four wheels down and make sure that your weight is centred again.

● As your front wheels lift off the ground, stretch out your arms and use them to balance. Roll along on your back wheels with your posture holding you in manual. Enjoy the feeling of rolling balance.

● Begin to shift most of your weight to your back foot, using your front foot for control. Transfer enough weight so that your front wheels leave the ground, but not so that you scrape your tail along as you manual.

● Roll along, keeping your feet in the ollie position with your back foot squarely across the tail and your front foot just below the front truck bolts. Visualise lifting your front wheels from the floor while rolling along.

Along with the ollie, the boneless is usually one of the first tricks that any new skateboarder will learn. Like the no-comply, the boneless is one of only a few popular tricks that does not involve the ollie. Learn this one on the flat and then take it to all manner of obstacles from mini-ramps to flat banks.

● Land with all four wheels down and bend your knees to absorb the impact of landing. Gradually stand back up on your board, using your arms to balance your ride off. Roll away.

● Once both feet are back on the board and over the truck bolts, it is time to release your grab. As you do so, prepare to fall back towards the ground and concentrate on keeping your board level in the air.

● As your jump begins to peak, bend your back knee, bringing your front foot back onto the board. Hold it firmly, or you won't be able to get your foot back on it. Make sure both feet are over the truck bolts.

● Hop off your planted foot when your board reaches waist height, maintaining your hold on the edge of the board. Jump as high as possible, letting your forward momentum guide you along.

● Balance on your planted foot, holding your board in your trailing hand, your back foot over the tail. Begin to lift your board upwards towards waist height and prepare to push up off your planted foot.

● Prepare to execute the boneless by crouching and visualising where you are going to plant your front foot. Take your front foot off the board at the heel side and plant it on the floor. Reach down and grab the toe side edge.

● Roll at a moderate speed with your back foot firmly on the tail and your front foot just behind your front truck bolts. It may help to hang your front foot off at the heel edge slightly.

no-comply

This is one of only a few street tricks that are not based on the ollie. The no-comply entered the skateboarder's trick vocabulary during the mid-1980s after being popularised by Ray Barbee, a famous US professional skateboarder.

● Visualise "scooping" your tail with the no-comply rather than the ollie technique. Roll with your back foot across the tail middle and your front foot just behind the front truck bolts, with your heel slightly off the edge.

● Step off your board with your front foot, leaving your back foot on the tail. As your front foot plants on the ground, your board will angle upwards, and you will need to control it by moving your back foot to compensate.

● Your board should begin to turn through 90 degrees as your front foot hits the ground. As soon as you feel your board lift up, guide it the right way by turning your shoulders in the direction that you want to go.

■　　▶　　　　　　　　set feet　　　　　　▶　　　　step　　　　　▶　　　scoop

● As your board almost rotates 180 degrees, jump up with your front foot and turn your body so that you are above your board and facing in the opposite direction.

● Bring your board level with your back foot and jump around, placing your front foot back onto the board towards the nose. Take care to compress the impact and use your arms to balance yourself.

● With both feet back on the board and placed over the truck bolts, ride away fakie. Turn your shoulders and begin to kickturn your way around so that you are facing forwards again.

● Ride away cleanly and think about what to try your no-comply out on next. There are many different variations of the trick that you will be able to tackle once you have mastered the basic technique.

▶ **hop** ▶ **land** ▶ **kickturn** ▶ ■

This is the most important trick in skateboarding today. The ollie was invented in the early 1980s by an American skater called Alan "ollie" Gelfand. Once you have mastered it, the potential of skateboarding really opens up and almost anything becomes possible.

● Foot placement is crucial with the ollie. Place your back foot on the edge of the tail and set your front foot just behind your front truck bolts. Practise setting your feet this way and rolling before going on to the next stage.

● As you roll, begin to bend your knees and crouch down on your board. Visualise snapping your back foot and tail against the floor while jumping upwards a fraction of a second later. This will help you master the timing.

● Hit the tail against the floor as hard as you can with your back foot. You will have to experiment to work out the precise details of where you place your back foot as everybody's ollie is slightly different.

● As soon as your tail pops off the ground, jump upwards. This crucial moment in the ollie will take some practice. As you lift upwards, angle your front foot and scrape it up the board, stopping at the nose.

● Now suck your back leg up while levelling the board out with your front foot. You must concentrate on keeping the board as level as possible in the air, with your feet positioned over the bolts at either end.

● As you level out in the air, your ollie will peak and you will begin to fall back towards the ground. Again, focus on keeping the board level at all times.

● Land with all four wheels down and bend your knees to absorb the impact of landing. Stay compressed until you are balanced again and rolling forwards. Then you can stand upright.

▶ **ollie**　　　　　▶ **level**　　　　　▶ **compress**　　　　　▶　　　　　■

shove-it

The flatland shove-it (or "push-it") is another basic street trick that does not require the ollie technique. This one is quite easy to learn and is used to form the basis of many more complicated tricks that you will come across later on in your development as a skater.

● Roll along with your feet set in ollie position but with your back foot hanging off the board slightly at the toe edge. This will help you to push your board through 180 degrees while you jump above it.

● Crouch and transfer your weight towards the tail, as you will make the board shove-it with your back foot. Feel the edge of your board with your toes and prepare to push down and out on your tail simultaneously.

● Keeping enough weight on the board to stop it flying away from you, push your tail with your back foot and jump above it. Only land this trick if you foresee the board turning through 180 degrees in a controlled way.

■ ▶ **set feet** ▶ **crouch** ▶ **push it**

● You should now be in the air above your board as it is about to complete its 180-degree rotation. Try to catch your board with your front foot when it has spun into the correct position.

● As your front foot lands on the board and stops it moving, bring your back foot onto the board and place it back on the tail.

● Compress and absorb the impact with your knees. Remember to balance yourself with your arms and shoulders.

● Straighten your legs and stand upright again, with your arms relaxed by your sides. Ride away, with your eyes facing forwards.

 jump ▶ **catch** ▶ **land** ▶ ■

fakie ollie

The basic technique for the fakie ollie is identical to that for the regular ollie. The only difference is that this time you are rolling backwards and therefore the timing needs to be slightly different.

● Roll along backwards at a moderate speed with your feet in ollie position. You may want to have your front foot slightly further down the board to aid the fakie pop. Look straight ahead of you and visualise popping an ollie.

● Crouch down as you would for a normal ollie. Pop your tail and jump upwards simultaneously. You must concentrate here as the timing for a fakie ollie can be tricky at first.

● As your tail pops and you begin to lift off the ground, scrape your front foot upwards as you would with a regular ollie.

■ ▶   **set your feet**   ▶   **crouch**   ▶   **pop**

● Suck your back leg up while bending your knees and levelling the board out in the air with the guidance of your front foot. Make sure that both your feet are on the board squarely over the truck bolts.

● As you feel your fakie ollie reach its peak, stay focused and concentrate on making a balanced landing. Keep the board under control, with the front angled.

● Land with all four wheels down and compress to absorb the impact of landing. Using your arms will help you to balance and stop you falling forwards as you hit the ground.

● Roll away backwards. Although the fakie ollie is a basic trick, it is quite difficult to get the hang of it because you are travelling fakie. Keep practising and it will soon get easier.

▶ **suck leg up**   ▶ **control**   ▶ **compress**   ▶   ■

For most skaters, the nollie is their first taste of switchstance skateboarding.

Learning to skate switch greatly increases your skating potential.

● Set your feet so that they are in the position for a fakie ollie but in the opposing stance. Let your front foot hang off the toe side of your nose and keep your back foot in the middle of the board.

● Crouch and prepare to pop. You must visualise popping off the nose and immediately sucking your back leg up, similar to the fakie ollie. Nollies are tricky to start with, but persevere and they will get easier.

● Hit the nose of your board off the ground as in any ollie-based trick. Use your back foot to control your ascent. You have to time your pop and jump perfectly here or you will not get off the ground.

● As you leave the ground, use your back foot to drag the back of the board upwards so that it is level with the front. This is the hardest part of the nollie. It will take some time to perfect before you pop a clean one.

● You should now be at the peak of the trick, completely level in the air, with your feet flat on the griptape. Keep an eye on where you will be landing and hold your poise.

● As you begin to fall back to the ground, pay close attention to keeping your weight balanced over both feet. Guide the board towards the floor and concentrate on landing with all four wheels down.

● Compress and absorb the impact by bending your knees. Make sure that your feet are over the truck bolts at either end to ensure that you land safely.

● Straighten your legs and return to a standing position as you ride out of your compression. Roll away.

▶ **level out**   ▶ **compress**   ▶ **roll away**   ▶   ■

180 ollie

The 180 ollie is the next step after learning the regular ollie. As with all tricks in skateboarding, the 180 ollie can be done backside or frontside and the technique is similar for both.

● Roll along at a moderate speed with your feet in ollie position. Visualise the process of popping an ollie and turning through 180 degrees.

● Crouch down as you would for a normal ollie and prepare to pop. Be ready to turn your shoulders as soon as you take off, so that you start to turn the first 90 degrees as you leave the ground.

● Pop your tail and lift yourself up. As you take off, raise your arms upwards and turn your shoulders so that you are at 90 degrees to your starting position.

As you reach the peak of your ollie, begin to turn the last half of your 180. You should try to land on your front wheels a fraction of a second before the back ones.

Land with both feet on the board and pivot round the last of the 180 with all four wheels on the ground.

Steady yourself with your arms and crouch to absorb the impact. Begin to stand up again as you start to roll out of the trick.

Roll away fakie. Keep practising so that your 180 ollies are as powerful and stylish as your straight ollies.

▶ **turn**   ▶ **pivot**   ▶ **land**   ▶   ■

intermediate

intermediate
50/50

The 50/50 is the most basic of all the grinding tricks that involve dragging the metal hangers of your trucks across a hard edge. The trick gets its name from the fact that both trucks are in contact with the grinding edge of the bar.

● Approach the bar at a moderate speed. Grinding requires momentum, so if you approach too slowly your trucks will stop dead on the bar. Set your feet in the ollie position and line yourself up parallel to the bar.

● Crouch and pop a big enough ollie to get above the bar. You must level out your ollie before making contact with the bar so that both trucks land simultaneously into the 50/50.

● Land on the bar, crouch and balance yourself as you lock into the grind. Make sure that both your trucks are fully locked into position.

● Lean backwards a little into the grind and stand up on top of it. Now you can enjoy the feeling of a controlled grind for as long as you can maintain your speed.

● Be aware of the end of the bar as you move towards it and shuffle your feet a little so that you can pop a weak ollie as you get to the end.

● Lean backwards onto your tail as your front truck leaves the bar but don't lean back too far. Make the motion of an ollie without popping your tail fully, and this should make you clear the end of the bar easily.

● As you come out of your grind, you need to make sure that your board is level. Land with all four wheels down and bend your knees to absorb the impact of landing.

● Straighten your legs, relax your arms and return to a standing position as you roll away.

backside boardslide

The boardslide is generally the first block or bar trick that any skater learns. Originally, it was a trick invented by pool skaters, but it was then taken to street obstacles using the ollie. Remember that boardslides require a certain amount of speed to make the bottom of your deck slide.

- Straighten up into a standing position and relax your arms by your sides. Roll away, contemplating your next boardslide.

- Compress slightly to absorb the impact and slowly turn to face the front again.

- Turn your shoulders as your board clears the end of the bar. Land with all four wheels down, travelling forwards.

- Pay attention to the end of the bar as you approach it. Visualise turning your shoulders and board back onto the floor.

● Distribute your weight evenly between both feet. Use your shoulders and arms to balance your slide and lean back slightly. Hold your position and slide the full length of the bar.

● Turn your ollie through almost 90 degrees so that you are slightly above the bar and prepare to balance yourself. Make sure that you are fully on top of the bar with your feet at either end of your deck.

● Set your feet in a regular ollie position and use your arms to help you keep your balance. As you near the bar, crouch slightly and bend your knees. Judge your move carefully as you begin to pop your ollie.

● Make sure that your run up is long enough to be able to approach the bar at a moderate speed. A short run up will not be enough. As you push towards the bar, focus on the point where you will need to ollie.

backside noseslide to fakie

The noseslide works on exactly the same principle as the boardslide; the only difference is the part of your board that you choose to slide on. As with the boardslide, you will need to approach the block at a moderate speed in order to make the noseslide.

● Approach the block at a slight angle with your feet set in ollie position. Visualise the point at which you will need to pop your ollie.

● Crouch down and then pop an ollie high enough so that you can get your nose completely above the block. Turn your shoulder as you pop and turn the board through 90 degrees.

● While in the air above the block, push your front foot down so that your nose locks onto the edge of the block. Press your foot down hard and turn shoulders back so that you are facing forwards.

● Lock yourself into position and stand on top of your noseslide while guiding the slide with your back foot. Concentrate on holding your position here so that your slide is controlled.

● As you get close to the end of the block, begin to turn your shoulders and back foot. Make sure that you keep this motion fluid so that you can land cleanly and smoothly with all four wheels down.

● Turn through 90 degrees as you feel yourself leaving the block and land clear of it. Compress to absorb the impact of landing.

● Return to an upright position, with your arms by your sides, and roll away, backwards, from the block.

The kickflip is the basic move that all other kickflip variations depend on. To be a proficient and well-rounded skater, concentrate on learning the basics before moving on to more difficult tricks. Focus on getting a clean flick of the board and catching the board in the air with your back foot.

● Roll at a moderate speed with your feet in ollie position. You will need to angle your front foot slightly with your heel off the edge and your toes angled towards the nose.

● Crouch and prepare to pop the tail. You need to visualise flicking your front foot up and out as you pop so that you flick the board with your toes, making it flip over.

● Pop your tail and flick upwards and out as you feel yourself leaving the ground. You need to jump upwards as well so that your body is above the board as it flips.

● Flick the edge of the board with your toes and watch it flip beneath you. Stay above the board, keeping both legs level to ensure that you will catch the board flat.

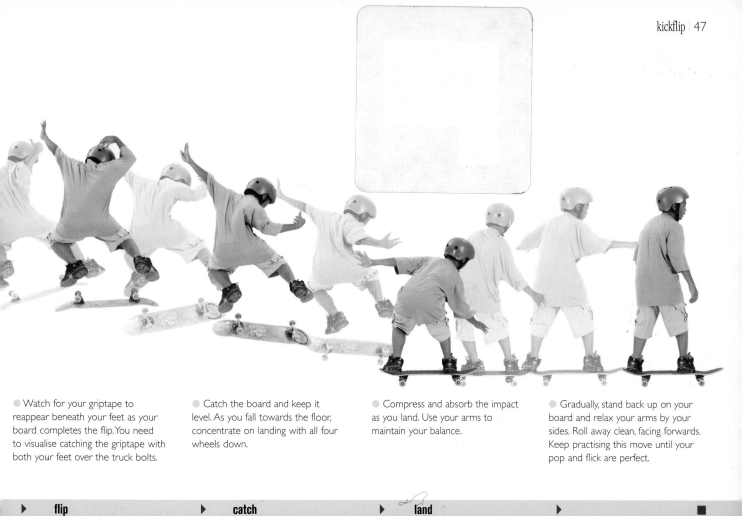

● Watch for your griptape to reappear beneath your feet as your board completes the flip. You need to visualise catching the griptape with both your feet over the truck bolts.

● Catch the board and keep it level. As you fall towards the floor, concentrate on landing with all four wheels down.

● Compress and absorb the impact as you land. Use your arms to maintain your balance.

● Gradually, stand back up on your board and relax your arms by your sides. Roll away clean, facing forwards. Keep practising this move until your pop and flick are perfect.

heelflip

intermediate

The heelflip is a close relation of the kickflip and is also the root of many more complex heelflip variations. The technique is quite similar to that of the kickflip, except that the board is flipped by the front heel and rotates in an anti-clockwise direction.

● Roll forwards with your feet in ollie position. Your front foot should be hanging off the side of your board along the toe-side edge. Make sure that your back foot is well placed to pop the tail hard.

● Crouch down and prepare to pop. Visualise yourself doing an ollie, and then kicking your front foot up and out to the side. This movement will pop the board into the air and start its rotation. Now try it.

● Hit the tail and flick the board with your front heel while jumping above your board. Keep your arms outstretched to help you balance.

● Stay above the board and try to keep level. Bring your front foot back towards the board as you prepare to catch it.

● Catch the board as the griptape reappears beneath you. Use your feet to keep the board level as it falls back to the ground.

● Compress your body to absorb the impact. Make a balanced landing, spreading your body weight evenly across both feet. Check that your feet are above the truck bolts.

● Straighten your legs and return to an upright position. Slow yourself to a stop with your back foot.

▶ **catch**   ▶ **float**   ▶ **land**   ▶   ■

pop shove-it flip

Also known as the "varial kickflip", this is basically a combination of the pop shove-it and the kickflip. The trick involves elements of both techniques and is a good place to start learning other kickflip variations.

● Set your back foot on the tail for a pop shove-it and angle your front foot into kickflip position. Roll on your board at a moderate speed.

● Crouch and prepare to pop your tail, scoop and flip at the same time. Visualise this process in your head as you prepare yourself.

● Pop the tail while scooping it around. As your board begins to shove-it, flick your front toes out and make the board flip as it rotates.

● The board should be flipping and rotating through 180 degrees beneath you at this point. Watch for your griptape to re-appear.

● As you board completes the flip, catch it with your front foot first. You need to catch it flat in the air so that you can get your front foot back on.

● With both feet placed over your truckbolts, guide your board back towards the ground and concentrate on keeping it level.

● Compress to absorb the impact as you land. Straighten up into a standing position and ride away.

▶ **flip**   ▶ **catch**   ▶ **land**   ▶

half-cab kickflip

Two separate tricks are incorporated in this variation to create the half-cab kickflip. You will first need to practise kickflips and half-cabs individually and then combine the two techniques.

● Roll backwards at a moderate speed with your feet set in ollie position and your front foot ready to flip your board.

● Crouch and prepare to pop your tail while turning 180 degrees and flipping. It helps to visualise this process before attempting it.

● Pop the tail and turn your shoulders through the first 90 degrees of your half-cab. As your tail hits the floor, begin your flick of the board with your front foot.

● As you peak in the air, you should still be at about 90 degrees, with your board beginning to flip beneath your feet. Try to relax and flip the board in a casual but powerful manner as this will help you to catch it.

roll fakie   pop   ▶   turn and flick   ▶   flip

● Stay above your board and wait for the griptape to reappear beneath your feet. Turn your shoulders as the board turns through the last 90 degrees.

● Catch the board with your feet over the truck bolts and guide it through the last few degrees of the 180-degree turn.

● Land with all four wheels down and your feet steady on the board. Compress to absorb the impact.

● Straighten up into a standing position and relax your arms. Ride away on your board, facing forwards.

▶ **catch** ▶ **land** ▶ ■

fakie kickflip

This is another variation of the basic kickflip. The fakie flip incorporates the techniques of the fakie ollie with that of the basic kickflip. As with all fakie tricks, you will need to master the timing, so persevere.

● Roll backwards at a moderate speed, with your feet in kickflip position. Visualise popping a flip and travelling backwards.

● Crouch and prepare to pop your tail, travelling fakie while flicking your front foot out at the same time.

● Pop the tail and begin to flip your board. Jump above your board so that it is flipping beneath your feet with enough room to rotate.

Stay level over the board and wait for the griptape to re-appear. Prepare to catch your board and make sure that it is level.

Catch the board with both feet and guide it back down to the ground. Concentrate on balancing yourself, using your arms, for landing backwards.

Land with all four wheels down, compress to absorb the impact, and lean into the ground slightly.

Once you are balanced, straighten your knees and stand back above the board. Roll away fakie.

▶ flip   ▶ catch   ▶ land   ▶   ■

Once you have mastered the flat-land ollie, you can take what you have learned to a kicker ramp. Popping an ollie out of the ramp at speed will give you much more height and airtime than doing it on the flat.

● Roll towards the ramp at a moderate speed, with your feet in ollie position . Now is the time to visualise the point on the ramp where you will need to pop your tail.

● Crouch and prepare to ollie as you ride up the bottom of the ramp. Stay crouched and maintain your focus as you roll up the ramp.

● Pop your ollie as you feel your front wheels leaving the edge of the ramp. Suck yourself upwards and use your momentum to throw you up.

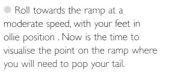
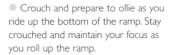

● Guide your ollie with your feet and concentrate on levelling your board out. Stay above your board.

● Keep level and balanced as you peak in the air and hold your position. As you begin to fall back towards the ground, keep focused and be aware of your landing point.

● Land with all four wheels down and both feet on the board. Compress to absorb the impact of landing.

● Straighten out your knees and body, and stand back up on your board. Roll away.

one-footed ollie

The one-footed ollie is a relatively simple ollie variation that can be performed on all manner of obstacles. Concentrate on popping your ollie high enough so that you are able to kick your foot fully off the nose.

● Roll along with your feet in ollie position. Visualise kicking your front foot off the nose of your board at the peak of your ollie.

● Crouch down towards your board and prepare to snap your back foot and tail against the floor.

● Pop the tail and ollie as high as you can. Take your arms out to shoulder height to help you keep your balance.

● As your ollie begins to level out, continue the movement of your front foot up the board and kick it off the end of the nose.

● Keep your board level with your back foot while you peak in the air, with your front foot off the board.

● Replace your front foot on the board as you begin to fall back towards the ground. Concentrate on keeping the board level.

● Crouch and land with all four wheels down, keeping your feet over the truck bolts. Straighten your legs and back, relax your arms by your sides and roll away.

 kick out   ▶ **level**   ▶ **land**   ▶ ■

advanced

frontside lipslide

Once you have learned the basic sliding and grinding tricks, you can begin work on the many variations. The lipslide is similar to the basic boardslide; the only difference is that you pop an ollie over the bar into the slide.

● Roll towards the bar at a moderate speed. Make sure that your feet are set in ollie position.

● Crouch down and get ready to pop an ollie high enough to get above the bar. Visualise landing on the middle of your board with your weight centred.

● Pop the tail and begin your ollie. Turn your shoulders so that your ollie turns through 90 degrees.

● As you reach the 90-degree point, land on the bar. Remember to lean forwards slightly, using your arms to help you keep your balance.

■ ▶ **crouch** ▶ **pop** ▶ **land**

● Begin the slide, paying particular attention to remaining upright and keeping your legs as straight as possible. Allow your momentum to carry you along the bar.

● Maintain your slide for as long as you can. Remember that the longer you slide, the more confident you will become with the trick.

● As you reach the end of the bar, begin to turn your shoulders and hips. You need to turn your body so that you land rolling forwards.

● Bend your knees to absorb the impact as you land. Use your arms to balance, then slowly straighten your legs and roll away.

▶ **slide** ▶ ▶ **turn** ▶ **roll away** ◼

frontside 50

This trick builds on the basic 50/50. Use the same technique but lean back slightly so that you land and grind on your back truck only.

● As you approach the block at a moderate speed, make sure that your feet are in ollie position.

● Crouch and prepare to pop your ollie while concentrating on landing cleanly on your back truck.

● Pop an ollie that is high enough to take you over the block and land in the manual roll position with your back truck on the grinding edge.

● Use your arms to help you balance and remember to lean back into the grind. Try not to scrape your tail, as this will hinder your grind.

● Lock yourself into the grind and allow your momentum to carry you along the bar. Maintain your balance.

● Keep an eye out for the end of the bar and prepare to centre your weight again as you come out of the grind.

● Shuffle your feet so that you clear the end of the bar, and level your board out so that you land with all four wheels down.

● Bend your knees to absorb the impact as you land. Balance yourself, straighten up and then ride away smoothly.

▶ **balance**　　　　▶ **grind**　　　　▶ **shuffle**　　　　▶　　■

feeble *advanced*

This is another variation on the simpler 50 grind. The main differences are the position of your body and the back truck on the grinding edge. Concentrate on locking into the feeble position, which is a combination of the 50 grind and the boardslide techniques.

● Approach the bar at a moderate speed and get your feet in position on the board to pop an ollie.

● Crouch as you get close to the bar and prepare to ollie high enough to get above the bar. You need to visualise yourself in feeble position beforehand, because locking into this trick can be difficult at first.

● Pop an ollie when you are parallel with the bar so that the back truck locks onto the bar with your front foot pointing down. Avoid leaning too far either way or you will stop dead.

● Your back truck should be locked into feeble, with your front foot pointing towards the ground on the other side of the bar. Lean onto your back truck so that you begin to grind. Use your toes to direct yourself.

■　▶　**crouch**　▶　**pop**　▶　**lock into feeble**

● Stay locked in the feeble position and feel yourself grinding along the bar on your back truck.

● As you approach the end of the bar, visualise lifting your front foot up so that you will hop out of the grinding position. This part can be quite difficult until you have mastered the trick.

● Guide yourself towards the ground as you feel your back truck leave the bar. Aim to keep your board level as you complete the trick so that you land with all four wheels down at the same time.

● Land your board and crouch to absorb the impact. Using your arms to keep your balance, straighten up into standing position and roll away.

▶ **grind**   ▶ **shift weight**   ▶ **land**   ▶   ■

frontside noseslide

advanced

This is the frontside version of the basic backside noseslide. Frontside means that you will be sliding blindside, facing away from your direction of travel. You will find it slightly harder to balance while sliding this way. Practise locking into frontside noseslide first so that you are confident with the technique before you attempt to perform the trick with speed.

● Level your board out and prepare to land with all four wheels down, rolling forwards. Land, crouch to absorb the impact, and roll away.

● As you near the end of the block, take the weight off your front foot and turn so that you pop out of the slide and return to a forwards position. It is crucial that you clear the block to avoid catching the edge and falling off.

● Lean into the nose and slide with as much speed as you are comfortable with. It may help to wax the edge of the block to improve your slide.

● Once you have locked into the noseslide and have begun sliding along the block, use your front foot to keep in position.

● Land on the block, and lock your nose onto the edge by putting most of your weight onto your front foot.

●Crouch and pop an ollie high enough for your nose to be level with the block. As you pop, turn your shoulders through 90 degrees so that you are at a right angle to the block.

● Approach the block with your body facing the sliding edge and your feet in ollie position. Visualise your point of take-off so that you will be able to lock into noseslide.

frontside smith grind

This is another variation on the basic grinding theme. The frontside smith is similar to the 50 and feeble grind techniques, with most of the emphasis on the back foot throughout. Practise and you will master this trick.

● Land with all four wheels down at once and compress to absorb the impact. Straighten up into a standing position and ride away.

● As your back truck leaves the block, lift your front foot and hop out. You must concentrate on keeping the board level in the air as you do this.

● Grind for as long as your speed allows. As you reach the end of the block, visualise making a weak ollie with your feet. This will lift you out of smith grind.

● Continue pressing down on your back foot while pointing your front foot slightly downwards. The technique is quite difficult to master, so practise it until you are confident about landing into smith each time.

● Land with only your back truck locked onto the grinding edge and your front foot pointing forwards and down. As you do this, shift most of your weight to your back foot so that you begin grinding.

● As you rise above the block, visualise landing in smith position. Your feet need to be perfectly weighted at this stage; otherwise, you will stop dead.

● Crouch and prepare to pop with your feet set in ollie position. As with all grinding tricks, your ollie needs to be high enough to get on top of the block.

● Roll towards the block at a moderate speed. If you go too slowly, your back truck will stick and you will not be able to grind.

pop ◀ **crouch** ◀ **roll** ◀

frontside nosegrind

This is another grinding variation that uses elements of the techniques of both the ollie and the nose-manual. Speed and balance are crucial as it is very easy to stick while attempting to nosegrind.

● Roll towards the block at a moderate to fast speed, with your feet set in ollie position. Visualise grinding on your front truck while balancing.

● Crouch and pop an ollie with the point where your grind will begin in your mind's eye. You will need to concentrate on keeping your front foot squarely over the nose when you land.

● Pop an ollie and point your front foot down so that you will land with only your front truck in contact with the grinding edge. You might find it helpful at first to visualise landing into nose manual.

● Land with most of your weight on your front foot and use your back foot to balance yourself. Your forward momentum should be sufficient for you to grind along the block on the front truck at a comfortable speed.

■ ▶ **crouch** ▶ **pop** ▶ **land**

● Use your arms and back leg to hold yourself in the nosegrind position and continue along the grinding edge for as long as your speed allows you to.

● As you get to the end of the block, decide whether to pop out of nosegrind by grinding off the end of the block (best for beginners), or by popping a nollie while grinding to get off before the end.

● As you feel your back wheels clear the end of the block, begin to level your board out in preparation for landing. You must lift your front foot as you come out of the grind to keep the board level.

● Land with all four wheels down and crouch to absorb the impact. Gradually straighten up into a standing position and ride away.

▶ **grind**　　　　　▶ **dismount**　　　　　▶　　　　　▶　　　　　■

crooked grind

The crooked grind or "crooks" is a variation of a nosegrind where you sit in the grind at a slightly crooked angle to the block.

As with the nosegrind, you really have to concentrate on learning how to lock your body position into the trick.

● Roll towards the block at a moderate speed with your feet set in ollie position. You should be almost parallel to the block on your approach. Visualise your movements as you prepare for the trick.

● Crouch and pop an ollie. As with the regular nosegrind, you need to land with most of your weight on your front foot, so be aware of this and make sure that your foot is over the nose.

● Land with your front truck on the grinding edge with your foot slightly weighted to the heelside. You need to lock yourself into this position, which is best described as a cross between a noseslide and a backside nosegrind.

● Put most of your weight onto the front truck and use your back leg to guide your grind. Avoid leaning too far forwards and use your arms to help keep you balanced.

● Sit in this position and allow yourself to grind for as long as possible. Keep your weight firmly on the front foot and stay balanced.

● As you come to the end of the block, prepare yourself to nollie out of the crooked grind. There is no need to pop a nollie – just make the movements of a nollie with your feet.

● Try to pop out of the grind as your front truck clears the end of the block. Make the motion of a nollie and your momentum should do the rest. Stay level in the air.

● Land on all four wheels, bending your knees. Return to a standing position and roll away.

▶ **grind**   ▶ **prepare**   ▶ **land**   ▶   ■

backside tailslide

This is probably the most difficult and most rewarding of all the sliding tricks so far. Backside tailslides are the yardstick of board control and style. Once you have mastered them, you're on the way to being a very competent skater.

● Roll towards the block at a moderate speed, with your feet in ollie position. Place your back foot on the edge of the tail so that you can get adequate pop and can control the position of the tail during the ollie.

● Crouch and prepare yourself to pop an ollie. At the same time, visualise being in backside tailslide position. You need to start your ollie as if you were going to do a backside 180-ollie.

● As you pop your ollie, turn your shoulders through 90 degrees, making sure that your tail is above the block. Guide your board through 90 degrees with your feet so that you are ready to lock your tail onto the block.

● Land with your tail locked on the edge of the block and point the toes of your back foot to control your slide. Make sure that you are locked in and balanced.

● Lean back slightly to assist the slide while continuing to put most of your weight onto your tail. Use your front foot to guide your slide.

● Slide until you begin to lose speed. As you reach the end of the block, turn your shoulders and hips so that you leave the block facing forwards. You can hop out by doing the motion of an ollie as you release your tail.

● Try to make sure that you land fully forward and balanced. Crouch to absorb the impact and keep your arms outstretched to steady yourself.

● Gradually straighten up into a standing position and relax your arms by your sides.

▶ **slide**　　　　▶ **pop out**　　　　▶ **crouch**　　　　▶　　　　■

backside kickflip

This trick is a combination of the backside-180 ollie and the kickflip. Pay particular attention to the point where you catch the flip in the air, as this will determine how cleanly you land the trick.

● Roll forwards at a moderate speed with your feet set in the kickflip position. You might find it helpful to angle your back foot slightly to the toe side while you pop.

● Crouch and prepare to pop your tail. As you do this, remind yourself that you are going to turn in a backside direction. Begin to swing your shoulders towards your backside as you start the trick.

● Pop the tail while flicking your front foot out to start the flip. As you do this, turn your shoulders in a backside direction so that your board turns and flips the same way.

● Your board now should be midway through the flip at a 90-degree angle to your original rolling position. Try not to flip through the full 180-degree turn, as this will weaken your control over the whole move.

● Catch the board with your feet as the griptape reappears beneath you. This is the crucial part: as you catch the board at 90 degrees, turn your shoulders to complete the 180-degree turn with your board on your feet.

● Land backwards with your weight balanced between both feet. You may need to slide your back wheels a little as you land to ensure that you have completed the backside-180 part of the trick.

● Straighten your knees and use your arms to steady yourself. Roll backwards until you feel well balanced.

● Kickturn around on your back wheels so that you are facing forwards again. Keep practising until you have mastered the flip-catch-turn technique.

▶ **catch**　　　▶ **land**　　　▶ **kickturn**　　　▶　　　■

tres flip

The tres flip is an advanced variation of the more basic pop shove-it flip shown on pages 50–51. The technique is effectively the same, except that with the tres flip, your board flips while rotating through 360 degrees instead of the 180-degree rotation in the pop shove-it flip.

● Roll forwards at a moderate speed, with your back foot on the tail and your toes slightly off the edge. Keep your front foot angled for a kickflip, but placed slightly further back than for a regular kickflip.

● The tres flip requires two distinct movements. Rather than popping the tail, you need to pop and scrape your tail with your toes while flipping the board with your front foot. Visualise what you want your board to do.

● Hit the toe-side edge of the tail off the floor so that the tail begins its 360-degree rotation. As you hit the tail, flick with your front foot so that the board also begins to flip.

● Your board should start to flip while turning, so you need to jump high enough above it to allow yourself adequate room.

● Watch for the griptape to reappear as the board completes its 360-degree spin and flip. Prepare to catch the board with your front foot first.

● Catch the board with your front foot to stop it rotating or flipping any further. Guide your board to a level position with your front foot and place your back foot back on the board.

● As you drop, make sure both feet are positioned over the truck bolts and the board is level. Land cleanly with all four wheels down at once. Crouch to absorb the impact, straighten up and roll away.

▶ **flip**　　　　▶ **catch**　　　　▶ **land**　　　　▶

nollie flip

The nollie flip is effectively a switchstance fakie flip, so it will help to visualise this as you learn the necessary timing and technique. Concentrate on perfecting your nollies before you start working on this trick.

● Roll forwards with your feet in nollie position and your back foot angled slightly to assist the flip. Mastering the timing required for the popping part of the nollie flip will take some time, so persevere.

● Crouch and prepare to pop a nollie with your front foot while flipping the board with the back foot. Make sure that you pop a decent-sized nollie, as this will help you to flip smoothly.

● As the nose of the board hits the ground, begin to angle your back foot. Flick the toes of your back foot along the end of your board and off to the heel side. This should kickstart your nollie flip.

▶ **roll**   ▶ **crouch**   ▶ **nollie**

● Once you have flicked with your back foot, jump above your board and make sure your feet are not in its path. Watch for the griptape to reappear beneath you and pause, ready to catch the board with your feet.

● As you see your board completing the flip, catch it with your front foot first. Guide your board so that you can replace your back foot and are level in the air.

● Land with both feet over the truck bolts and all four wheels down at once. Crouch to absorb the impact and use your arms for balance.

● Slowly straighten your knees and stand back up on your board. Roll away victorious.

▶ flip ▶ catch ▶ land ▶ ❚❚

nollie heelflip

This is the heelflip variation of the nollie flip shown on the previous page. As with the nollie flip, it may help to visualise doing a switchstance fakie heelflip in order to understand the timing needed for this trick.

● Roll forwards with your front foot in nollie position and your back foot just above the back truck bolts, angled for a heelflip. Remember that a clean and stylish nollie heelflip requires a popped nollie.

● Crouch and prepare to pop a nollie. Visualise the process of popping, jumping and heelflipping with your back foot as you approach.

● Hit the nose off the floor and flick your back foot out towards the heel-side edge of your tail. This should cause the board to start heelflipping beneath you.

● Stay above your board and try to stay level in the air at this point. Ideally, your board should be rotating in a controlled manner.

● As you see the griptape reappear beneath you, catch the board with both feet. Try to position your feet over the truck bolts at either end. As you catch your nollie heelflip, make sure that the board remains level.

● Land with all four wheels down at once, making sure that your feet are firmly over the truck bolts. Crouch to absorb the impact.

● Balance yourself with your arms and begin to straighten up into a standing position as you roll away.

▶ **heelflip**   ▶ **catch**   ▶ **land**   ▶   ■

indy grab

Once you have mastered your repertoire of flatland moves, you can move on to jump ramp or kicker tricks. The "indy grab" was invented by Duane Peters. The jump ramp gives your ollie more height and distance, so you really have the air-time to perfect and contort your grab.

● Approach the jump ramp at a moderate speed, with your feet in ollie position. You will need to travel much faster when skating ramps to enable you to boost yourself into the air.

● Make sure that you hit the bottom of the ramp in a centred position. As you ride up the ramp, visualise the point of take-off. Crouch down and prepare to pop an ollie.

● Pump up the ramp until you feel your front wheels leave the surface. As this happens, pop your tail and throw yourself up and forwards into an ollie.

● Guide your ollie to its peak by using your front foot to level the board out at the highest point. As you do this, you need to bring your trailing hand down towards the toe-side edge of your board, ready to grab it.

● Grab the board at the highest point of your ollie and straighten your front leg while bending your back leg. This will cause your board to poke downwards at the nose and is known as "tweaking" your grab.

● The "tweak" must be fast and at the peak of the ollie. Release your grab as you feel yourself falling back towards the ground. Time this well to avoid landing with too much weight on the front of your board.

● As you drop, concentrate on keeping your board level. Remember that you will need to absorb much more impact, as you will be falling from a greater height.

● Land with all four wheels down at once and lean to control your landing. Stand up and ride away.

▶ **tweak**　　　　▶ **release**　　　　▶ **land**　　　　▶ ■

melancholy

The basic technique for the melancholy, or "backside grab," is similar to that of the indy grab. Here, grab the board with your leading hand on the heel-side of the board.

● Roll towards the ramp at a moderate speed with your feet in ollie position. Make sure you line up your approach so that you hit the centre of the ramp. Visualise your point of take-off as you approach.

● As you near the start of the ramp, begin to crouch down and prepare to pop an ollie.

● Pop your tail as the front wheels leave the ramp. Throw your body weight into the ollie while consciously bringing your leading hand behind your front foot, ready to grab backside.

● Guide your ollie to its peak using your front foot while sucking your back leg up at the same time. At the peak, grab the heel side of your board with your leading hand.

● Grasp your board firmly and straighten your front leg to "tweak" your melancholy. You need to fold your back leg into your chest as you do this to ensure that your board remains level in the air.

● Release your grab as you feel yourself beginning to fall back towards the ground. You must also straighten your back leg a little as you do this so you land with all four wheels down at the same time.

● Land level and crouch to absorb the impact. Use your arms to help keep your balance.

● Straighten up into a standing position on your board once you feel stable.

▶ **tweak**　　　　▶ **release**　　　　▶ **land**　　　　▶ ■

tailgrab *advanced*

The tailgrab involves an identical technique to the other two grabs shown on pages 86–87 and 88–89. In this variation, you need to grab your tail with your trailing hand. It will help if you try to visualise this as you approach the jump ramp.

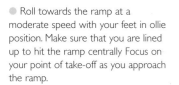

- Roll towards the ramp at a moderate speed with your feet in ollie position. Make sure that you are lined up to hit the ramp centrally Focus on your point of take-off as you approach the ramp.

- Begin to crouch and prepare your ollie as you roll towards the start of the jump ramp. Your feet need to be set up perfectly at this point as it is extremely difficult to adjust them as you roll up the ramp.

- Pop your ollie as your front wheels leave the surface of the ramp and launch your body weight upwards. Guide your ollie to its peak with your front foot while sucking up your back foot into your chest.

- Avoid letting your back foot trail or it will be much more difficult for you to grab the tail. Reach for the board and grab your tail firmly across the middle.

| ■ ▶ roll | crouch | ▶ pop | ▶ grab |

● Tweak by straightening your front foot. Maintain your tailgrab until you feel yourself beginning to fall back to the ground. Release your tail and begin to straighten your back leg so that your board remains level in the air.

● Land with all four wheels down at once, making sure that your weight is spread evenly across both feet. Crouch to absorb the impact.

● Gradually straighten your knees and stand up on your board, using your upper body to balance yourself.

● Come to a stop by skidding your tail along the floor. Kick the board into your hand and then repeat the trick with added confidence.

▶ **tweak**　　　▶ **crouch**　　　▶ **roll**　　　▶　　■

kickflip melancholy

This is a combination of the kickflip and ollie grab techniques covered in the previous three tricks. The emphasis is on popping a perfect flip out of the jump ramp and then catching it with your feet and leading hand simultaneously.

● Approach the jump ramp at a moderate speed with your feet in kickflip position. Make sure that your line of approach takes you directly up the centre of the ramp, as this trick requires perfect timing and execution of the pop and flick.

● Crouch and prepare to kickflip as you near the bottom of the ramp. You must visualise popping your flip as high and as cleanly as possible to make it easier to grab at the peak moment.

● Ride up the centre of the ramp and pop your tail as your front wheels leave the surface. Flick your front foot firmly and propel yourself upwards. Remember that a slow rotation of the flip will help you catch the board.

● As your board begins its flip, make sure that you are hovering above it, with your leading hand in place to catch the board behind your front foot on the heel-side edge.

■ ▶ **crouch** ▶ **pop** ▶ **flip**

● As you see the grip tape reappear beneath you, place your hand where you expect your board to be and grab. Catch the board with your feet almost simultaneously. Straighten your front leg to "tweak" the trick.

● Release your grab as you begin to lose momentum and fall towards the ground. Pay close attention to the position of your feet and focus on keeping the board level.

● Straighten your back leg a little to level the board out as you fall towards the ground. Use your upper body to centre your body weight over both feet. Land on all four wheels and crouch to absorb the impact.

● Gradually stand upright on your board as you regain control and slow yourself to a stop by skidding your tail.

▶ **catch and tweak**　　　▶ **release**　　　▶ **land**　　　▶ ■

index